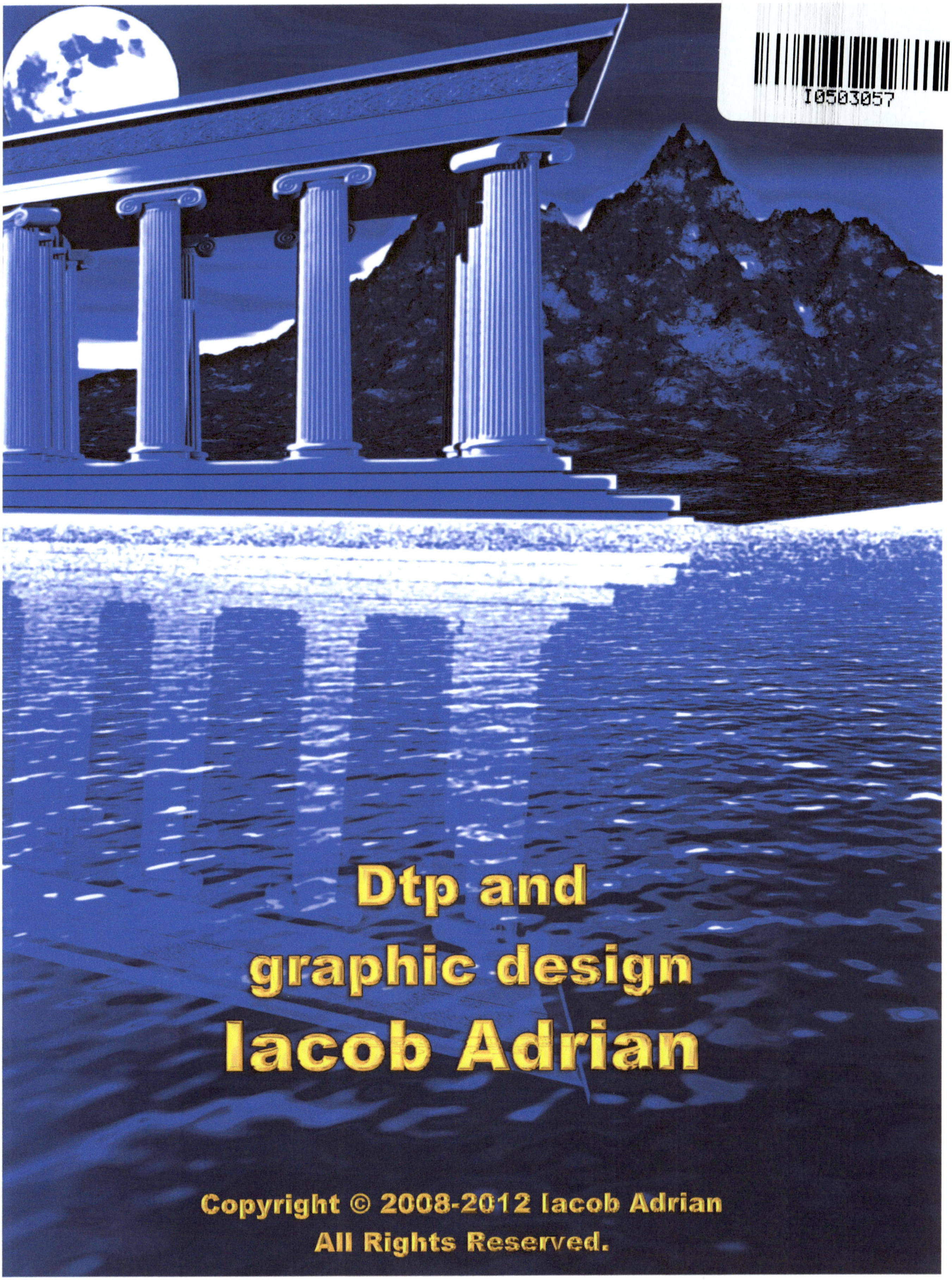

Dtp and graphic design

Iacob Adrian

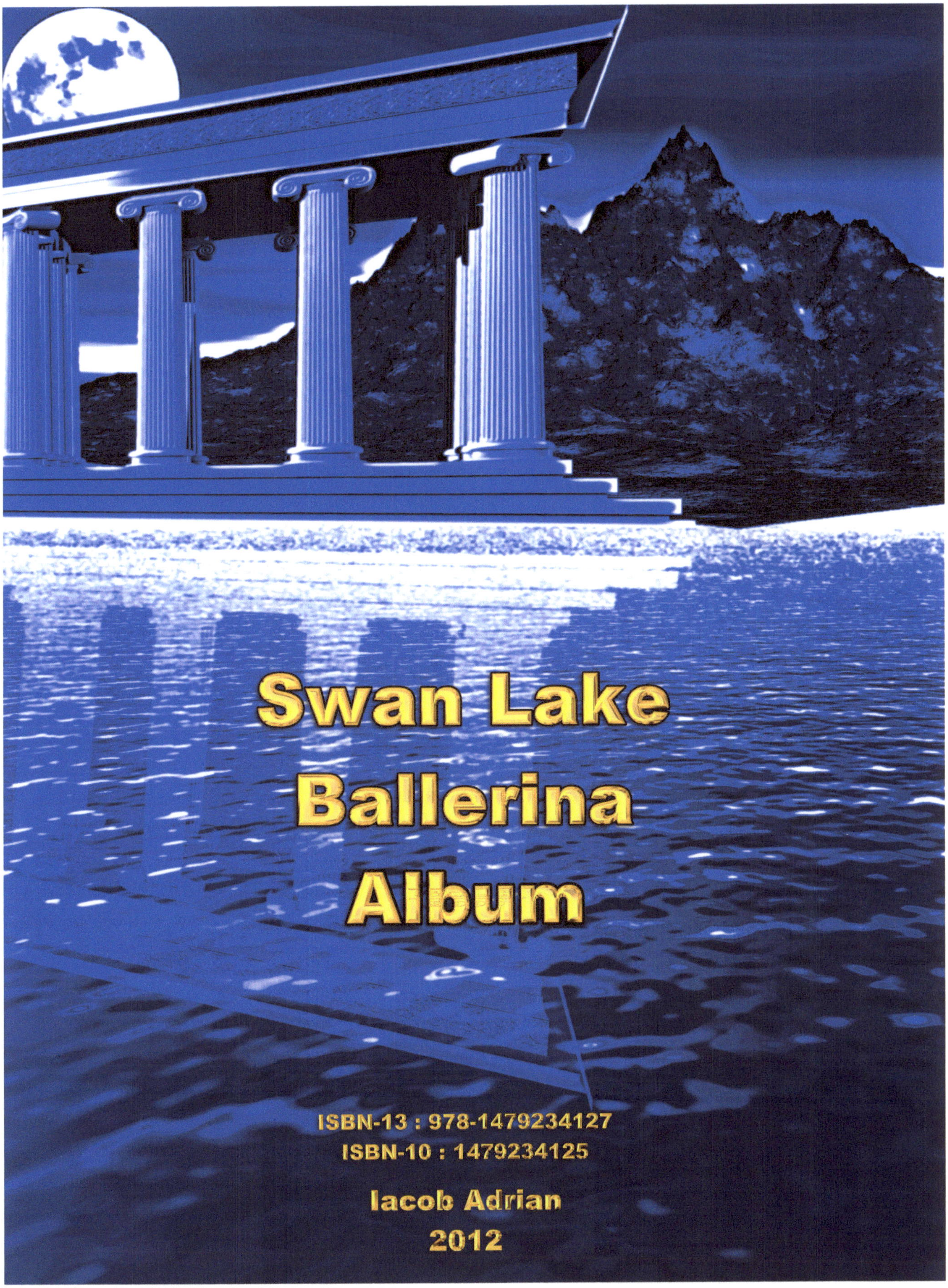

Swan Lake Ballerina Album

ISBN-13 : 978-1479234127
ISBN-10 : 1479234125

Iacob Adrian

2012

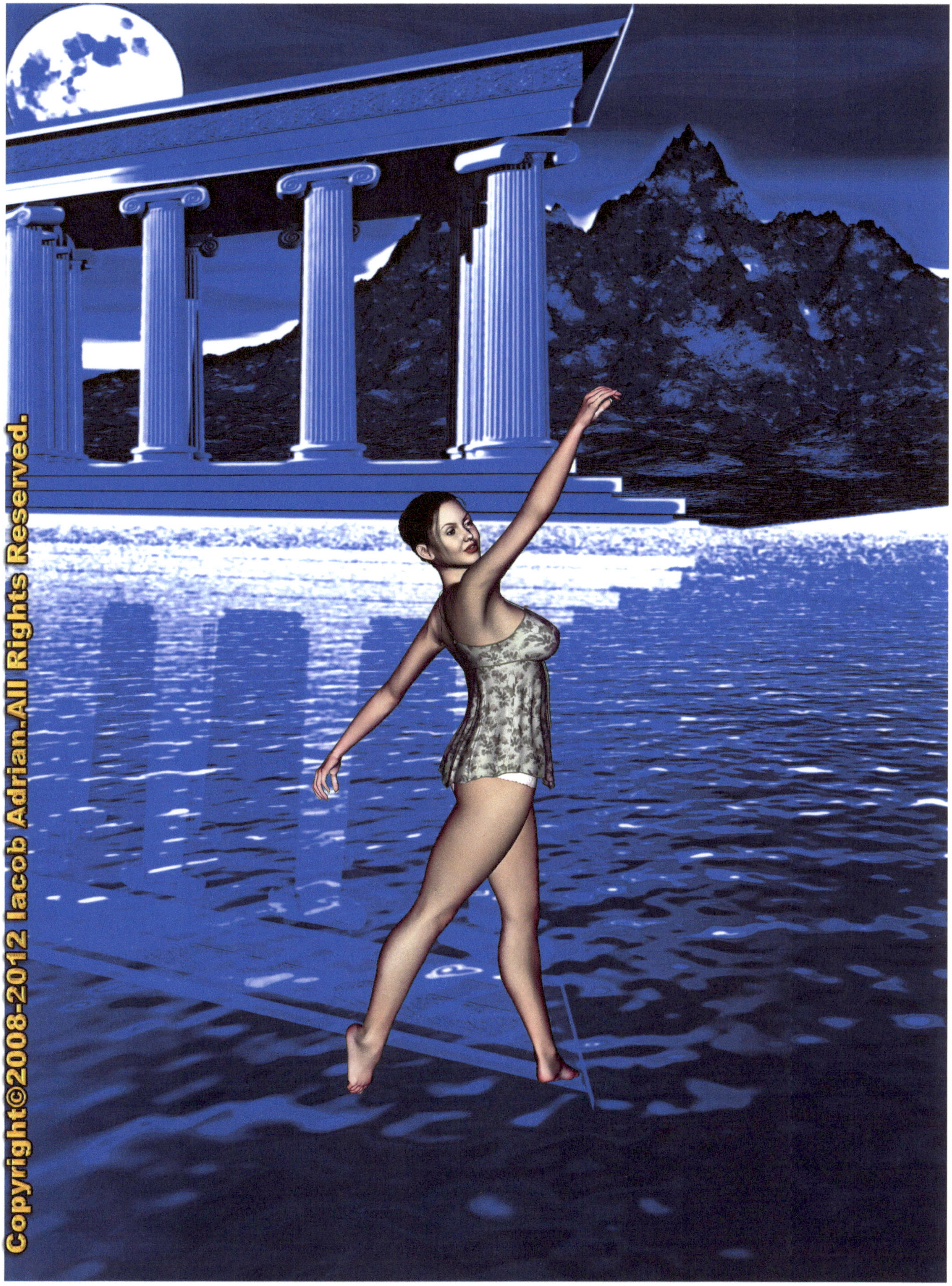

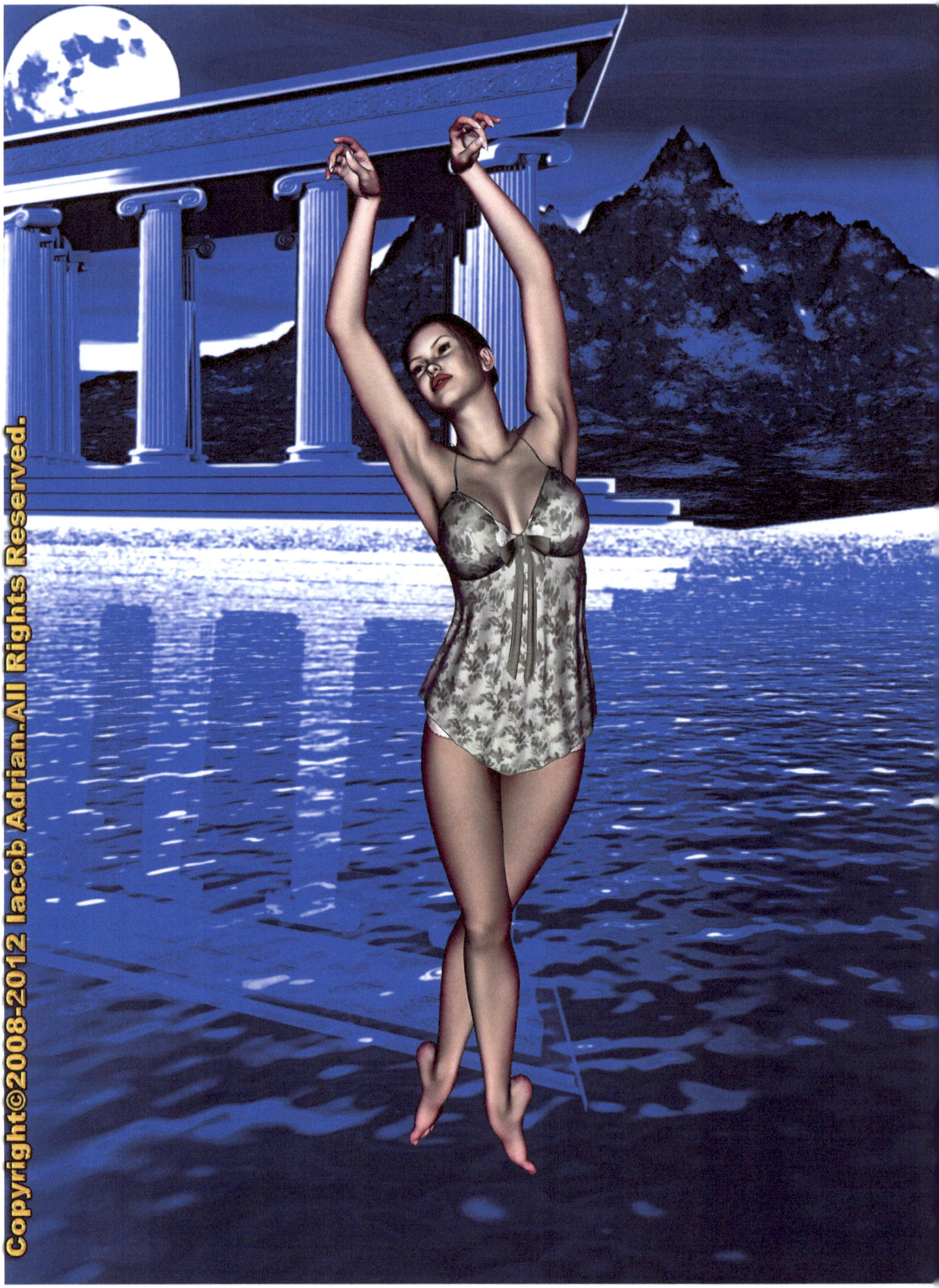
Copyright©2008-2012 Iacob Adrian-All Rights Reserved.

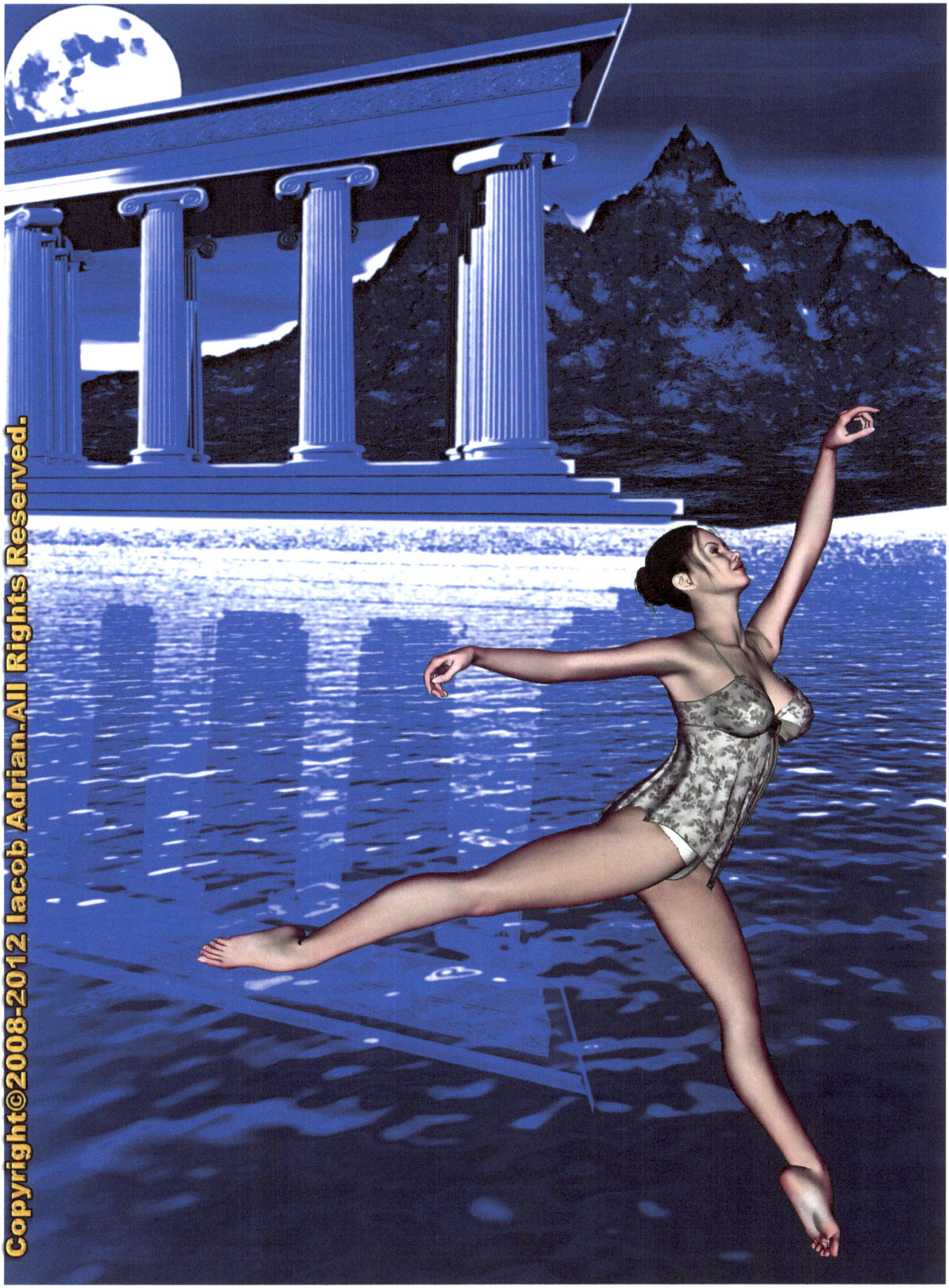
Copyright©2008-2012 Iacob Adrian-All Rights Reserved.

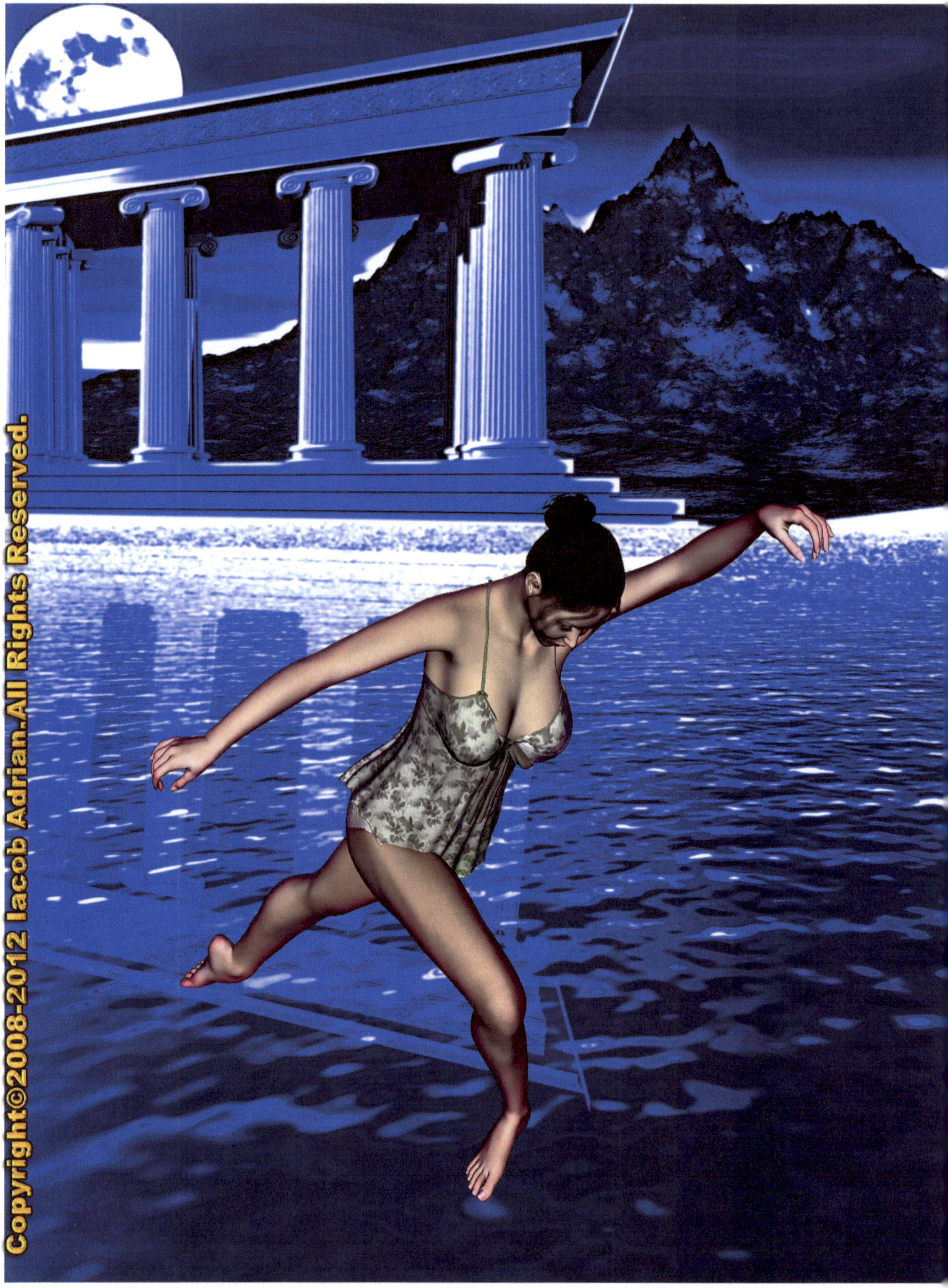
Copyright©2008-2012 Iacob Adrian.All Rights Reserved.

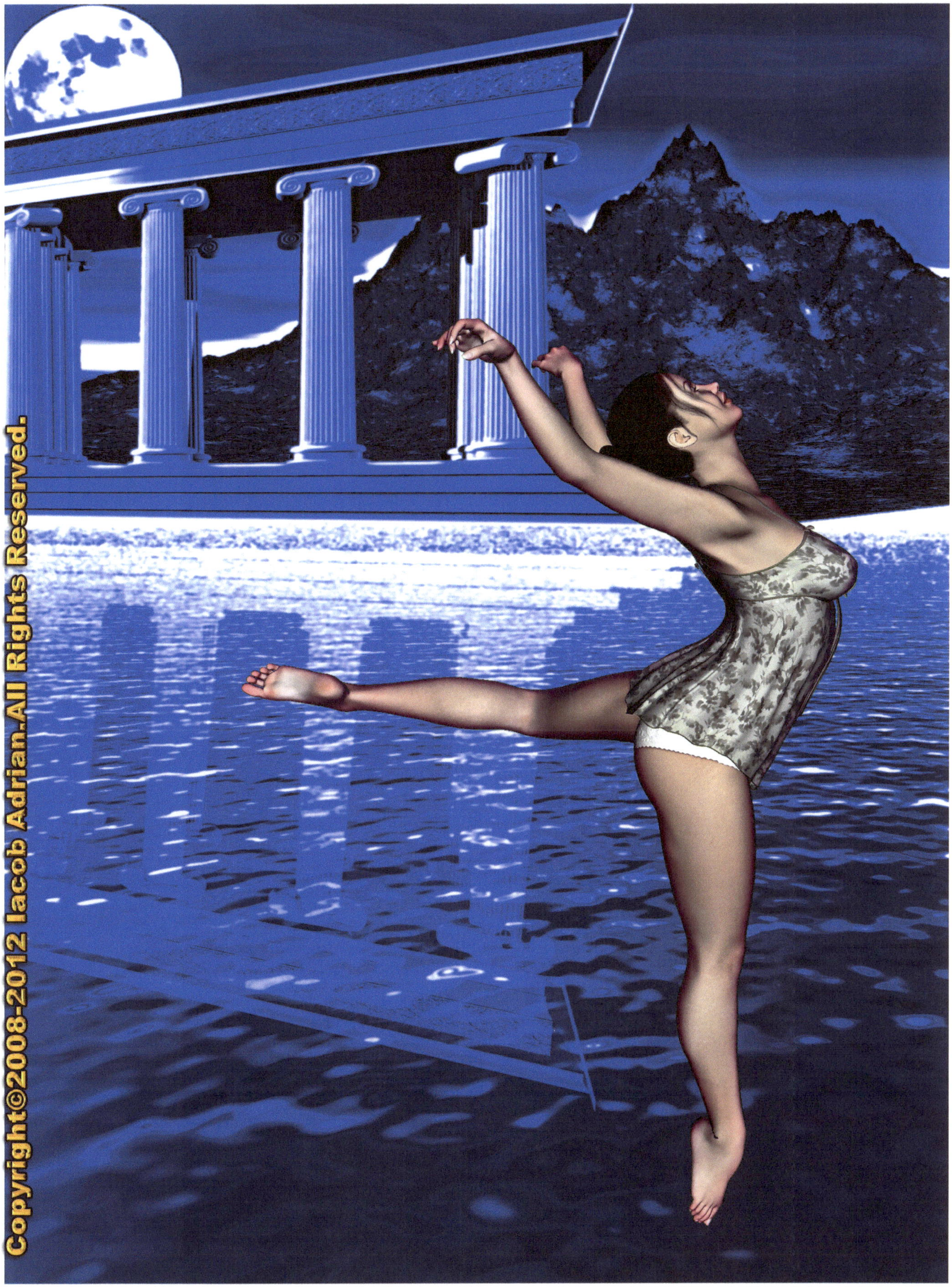

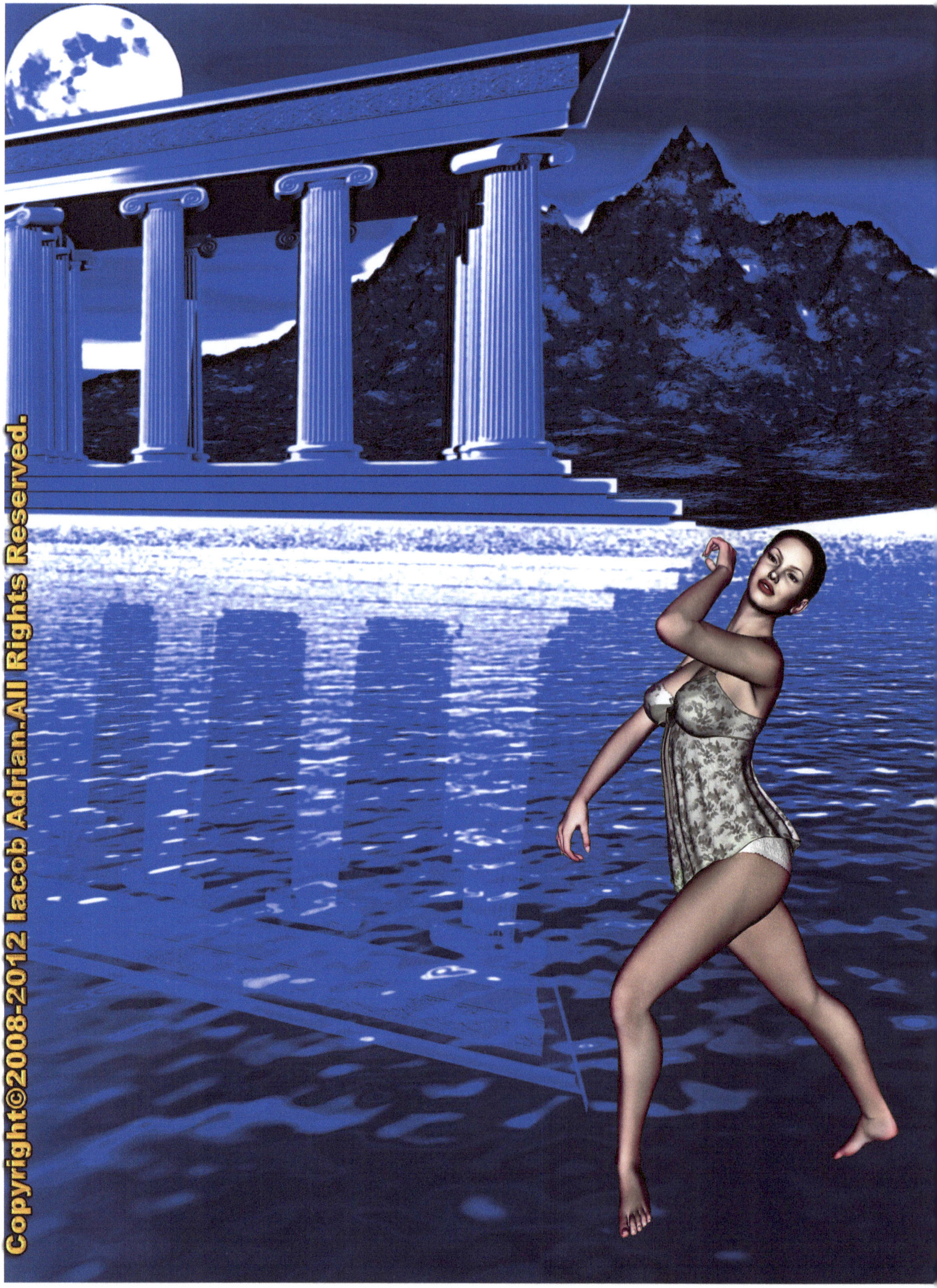
Copyright©2008-2012 Iacob Adrian.All Rights Reserved.

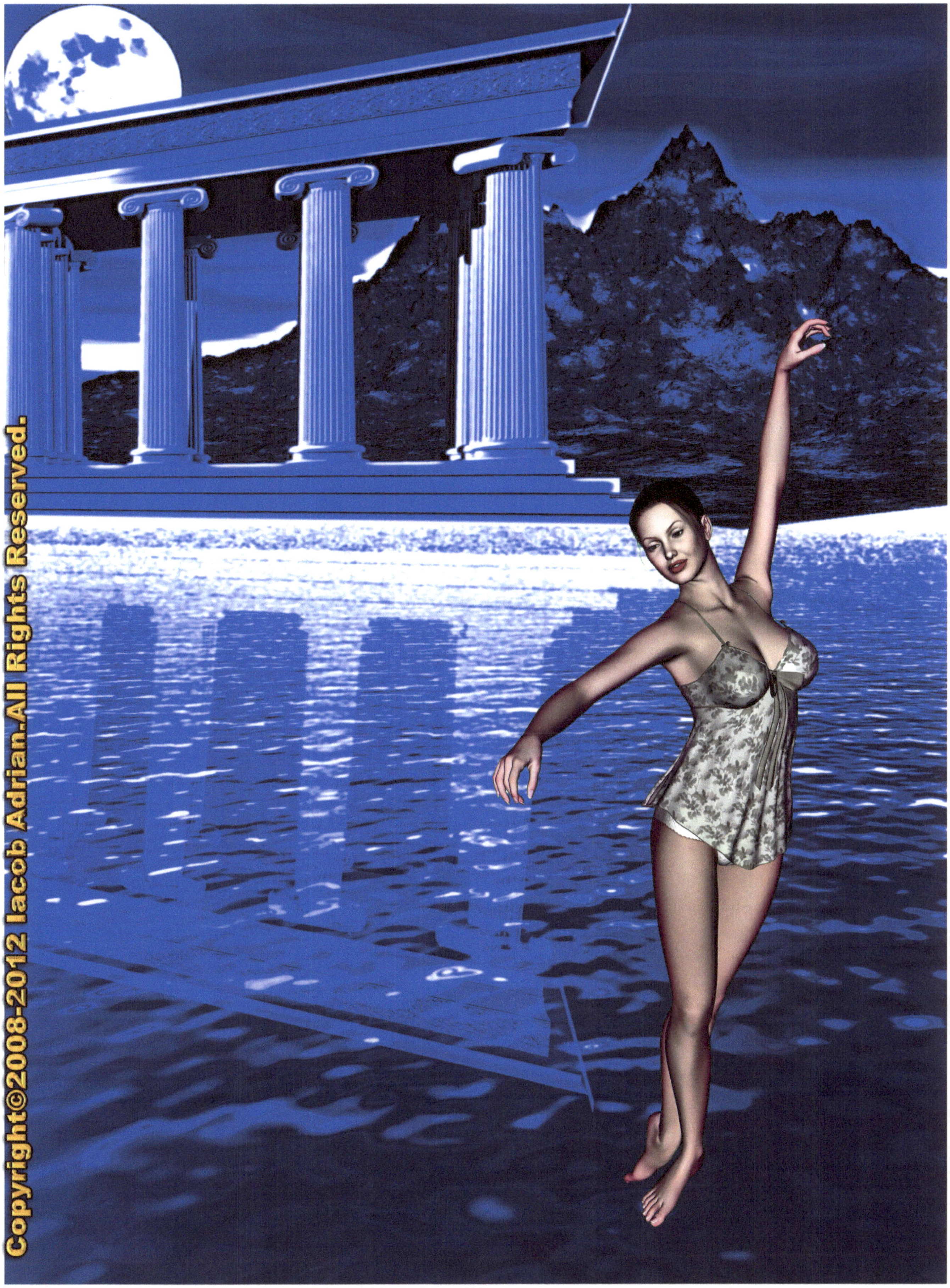
Copyright©2008-2012 Iacob Adrian.All Rights Reserved.

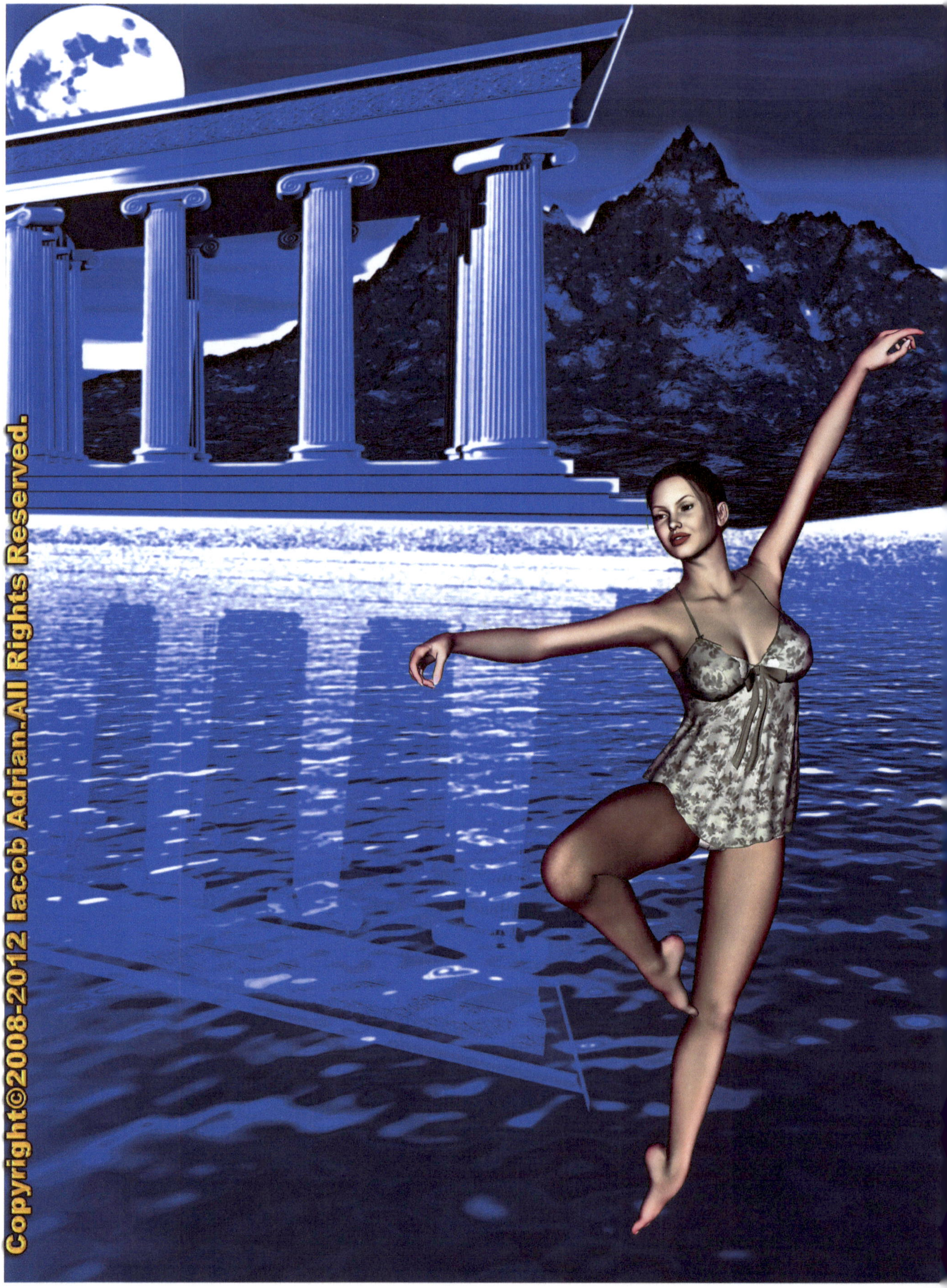
Copyright©2008-2012 Iacob Adrian.All Rights Reserved.

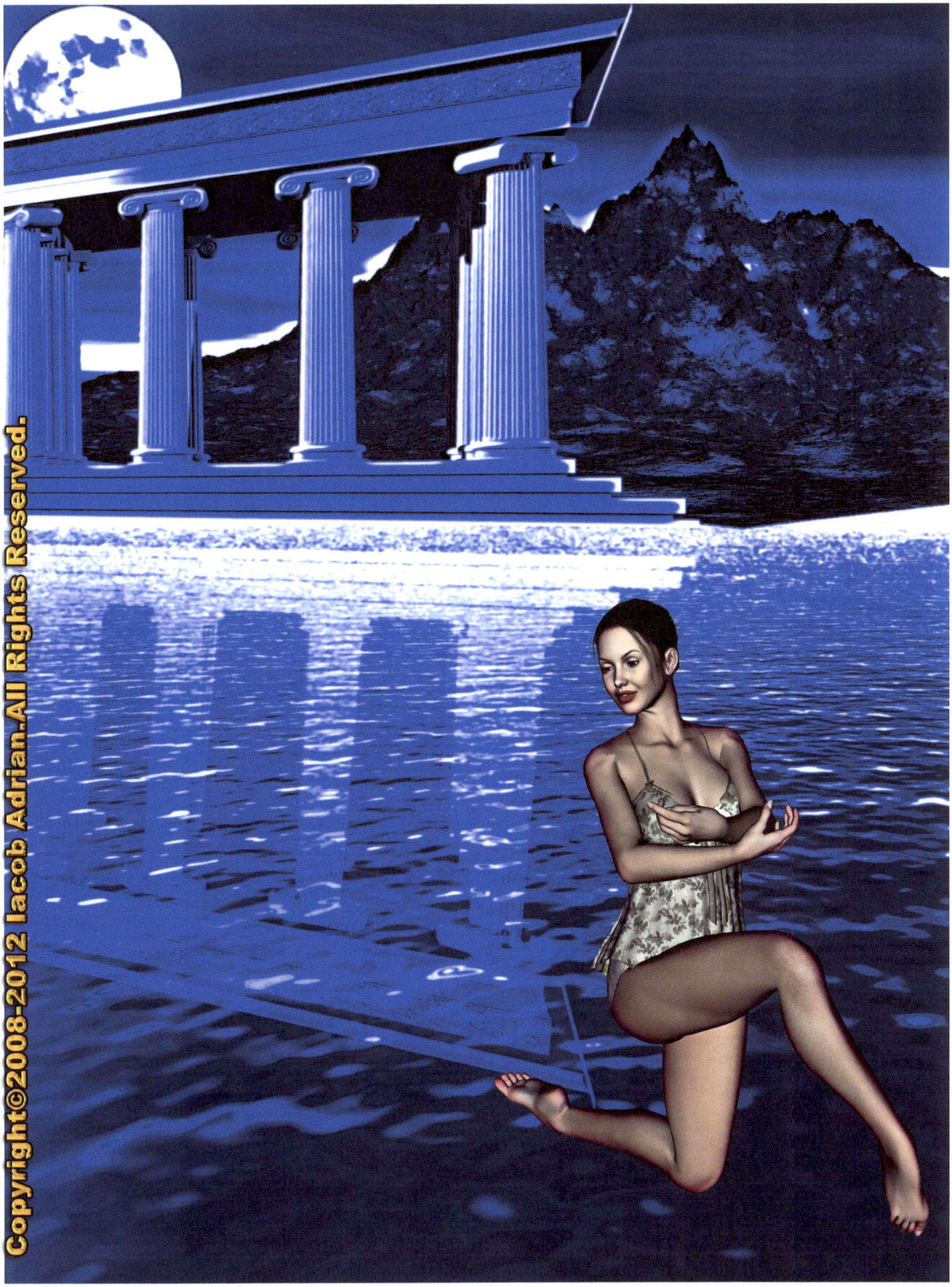
Copyright©2008-2012 Iacob Adrian.All Rights Reserved.

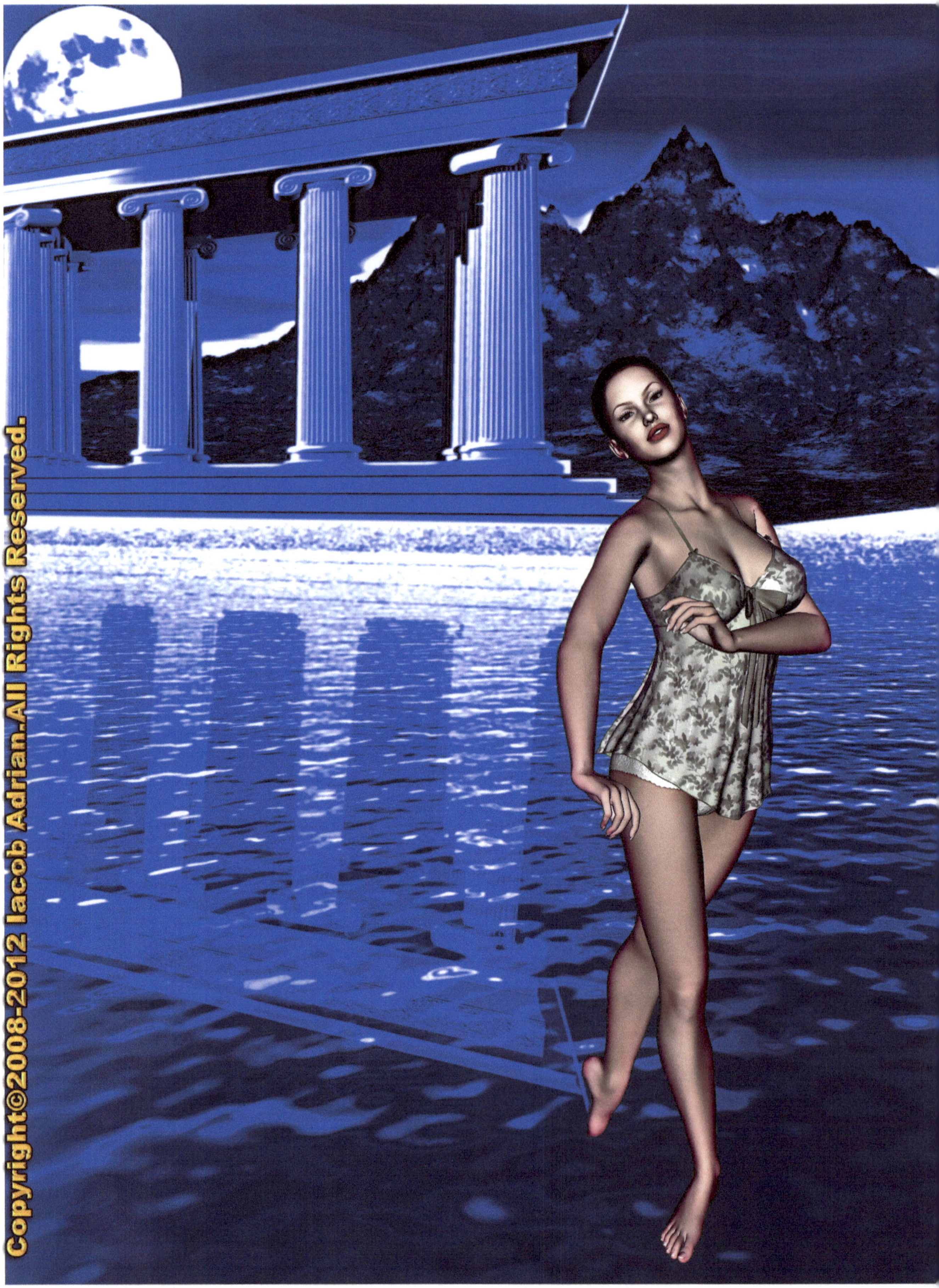
Copyright©2008-2012 Iacob Adrian.All Rights Reserved.

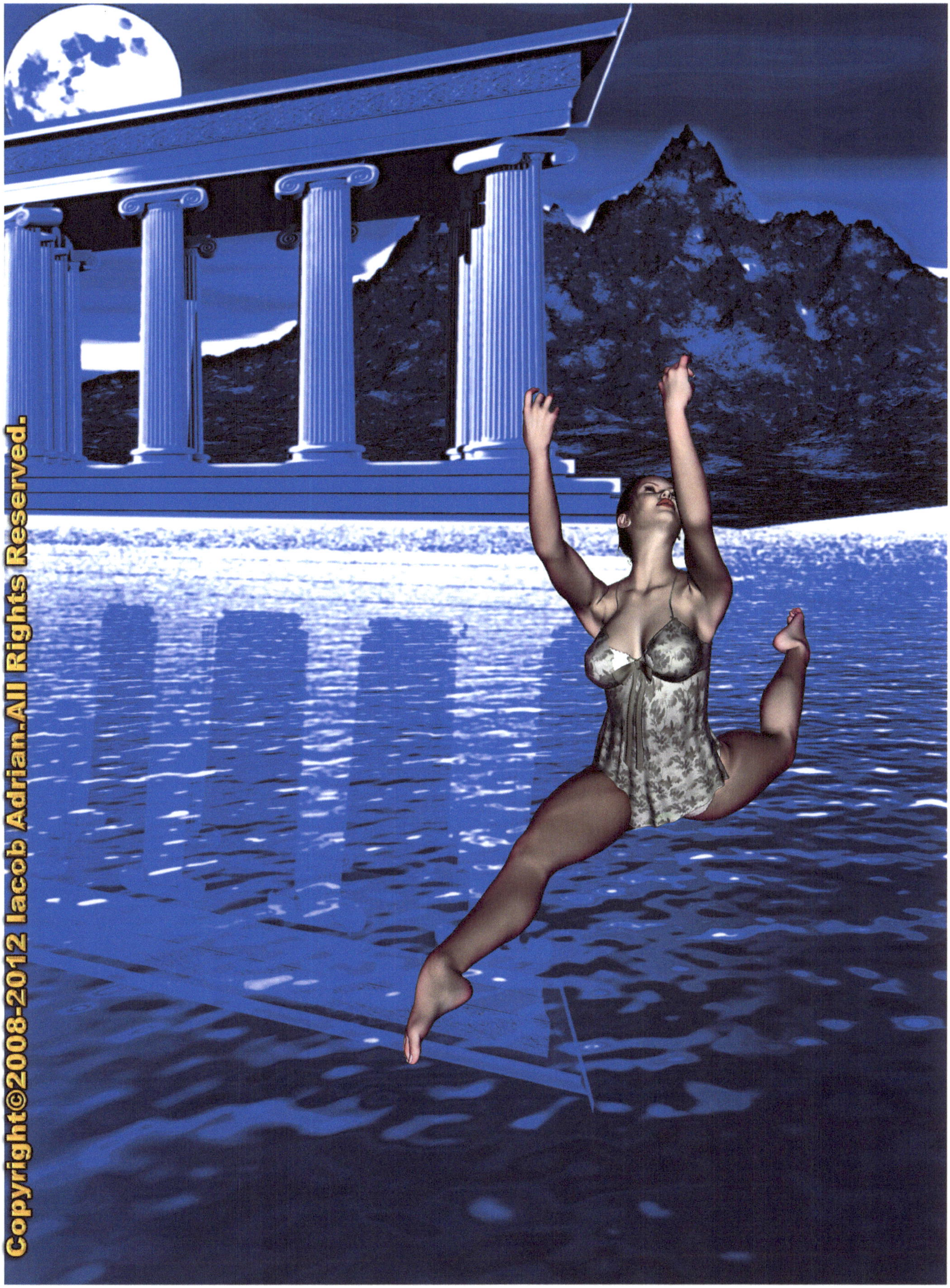
Copyright©2008-2012 Iacob Adrian.All Rights Reserved.

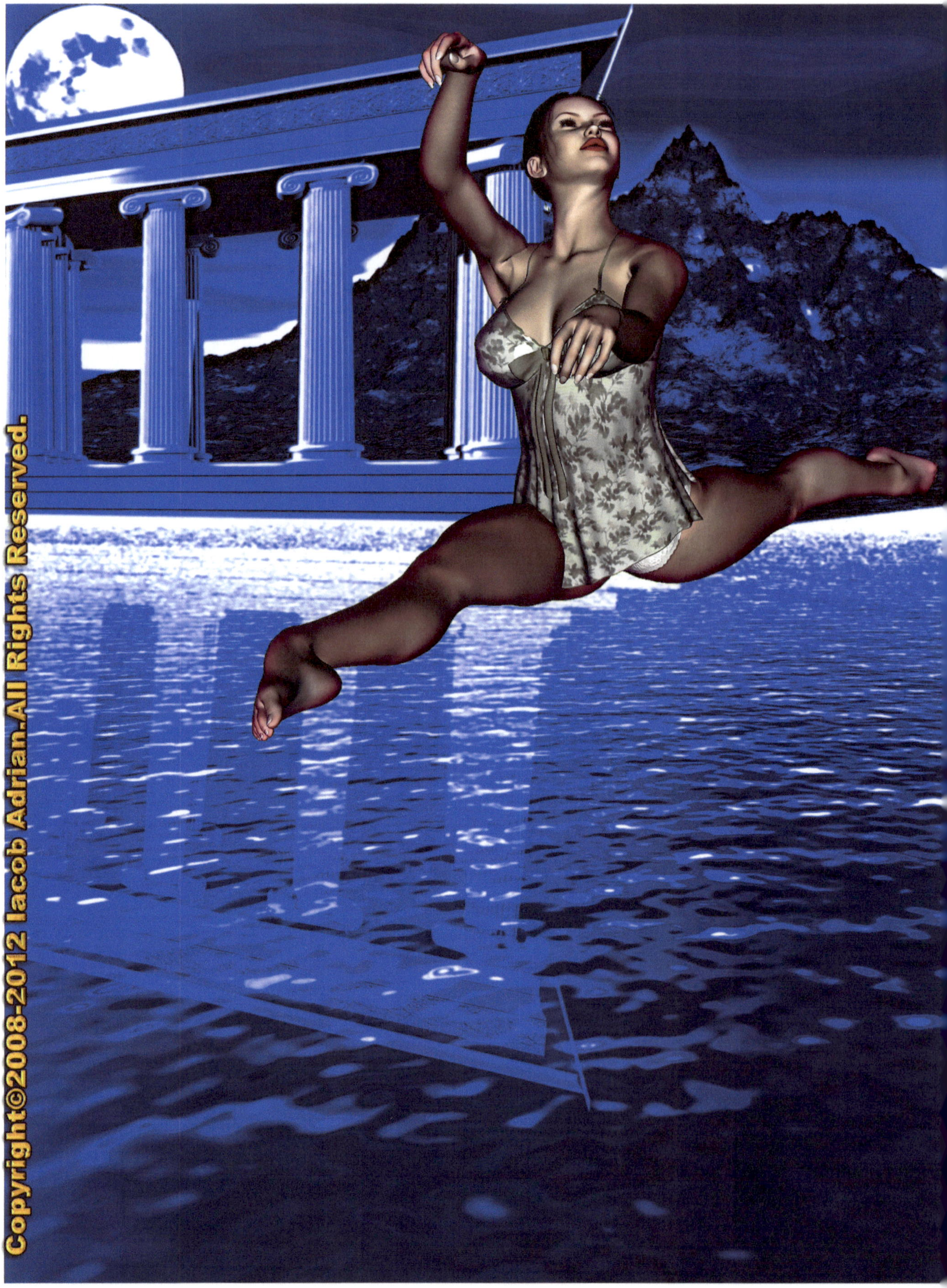
Copyright©2008-2012 Iacob Adrian-All Rights Reserved.

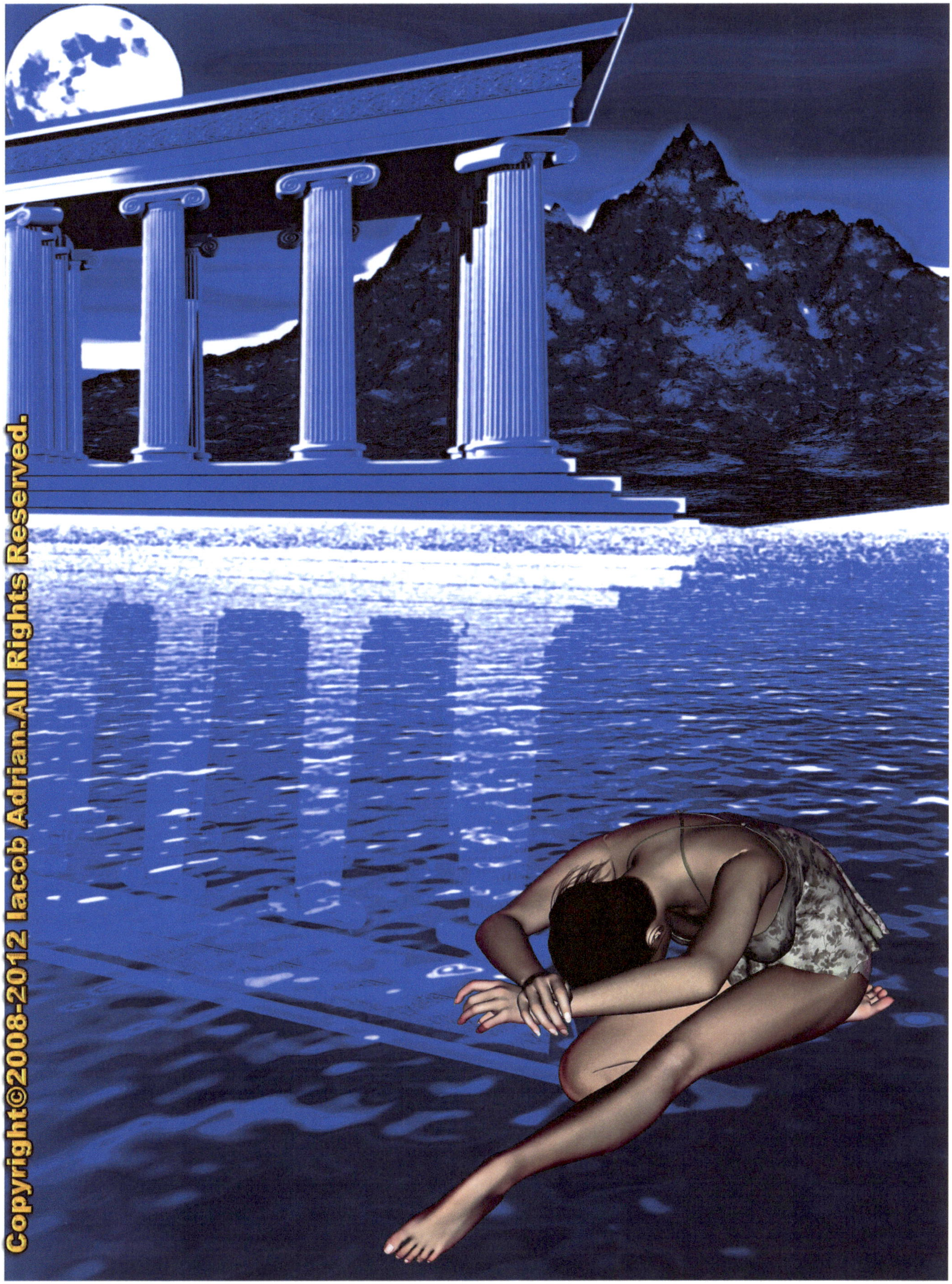

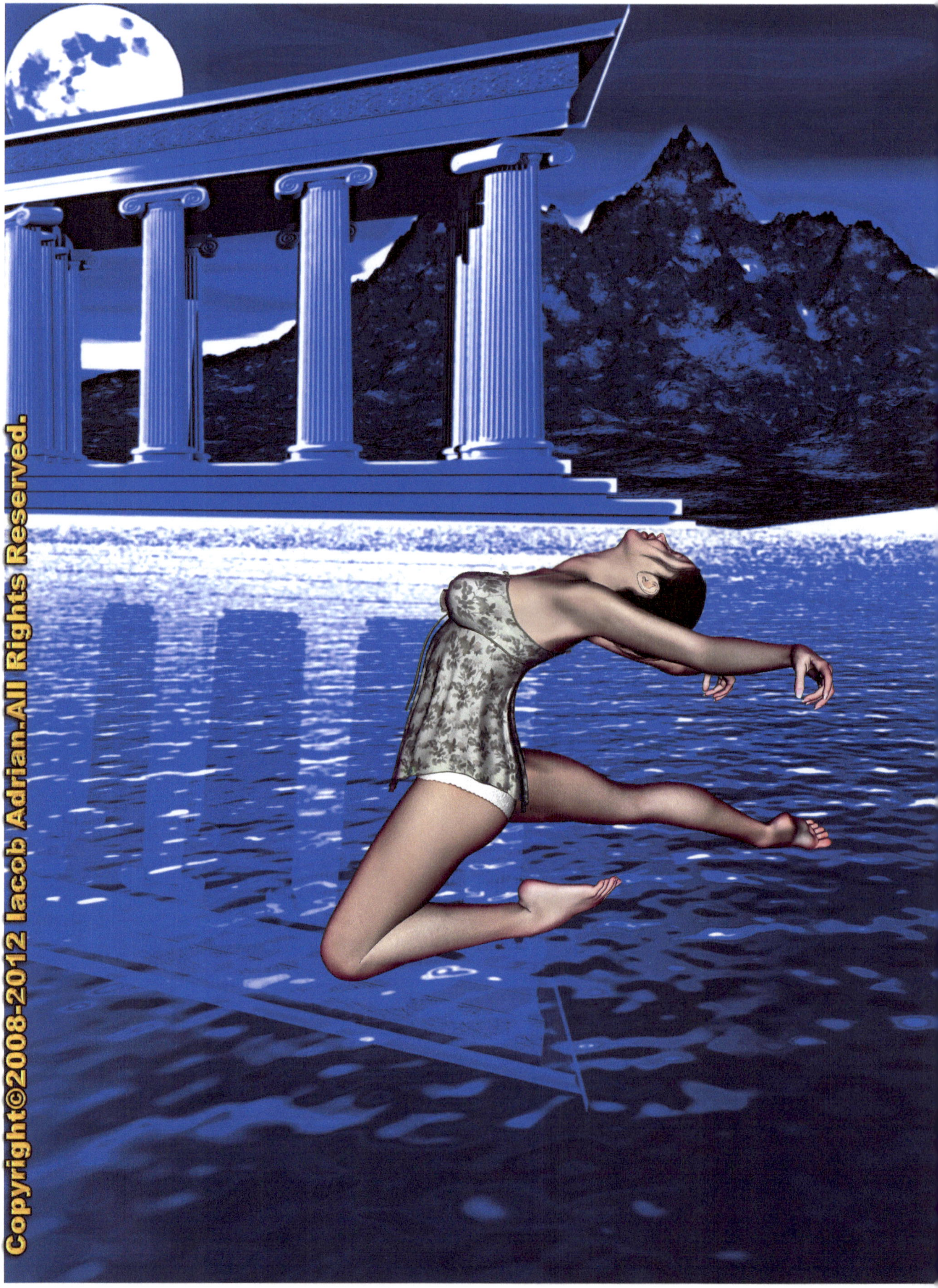
Copyright©2008-2012 Iacob Adrian.All Rights Reserved.

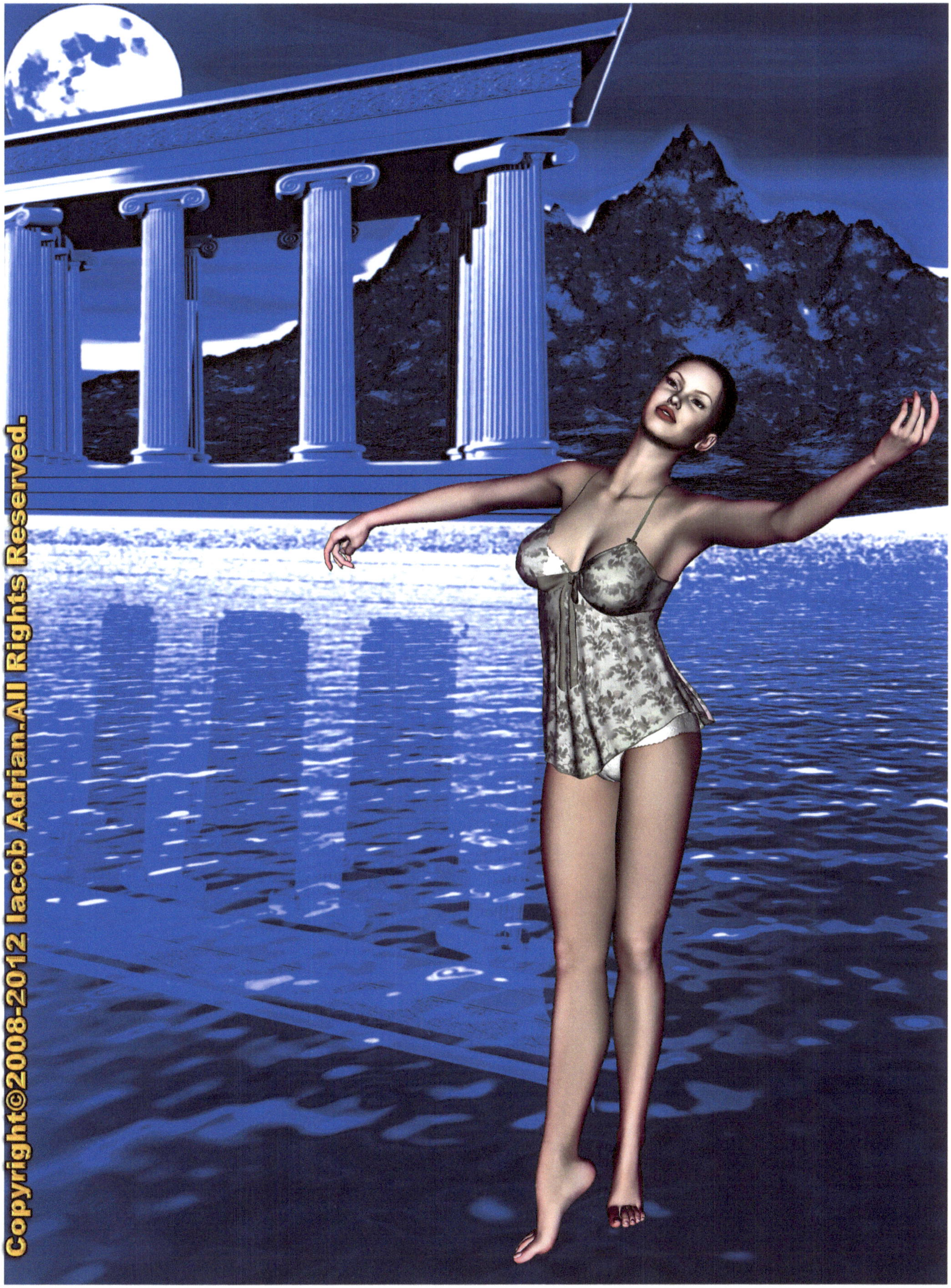

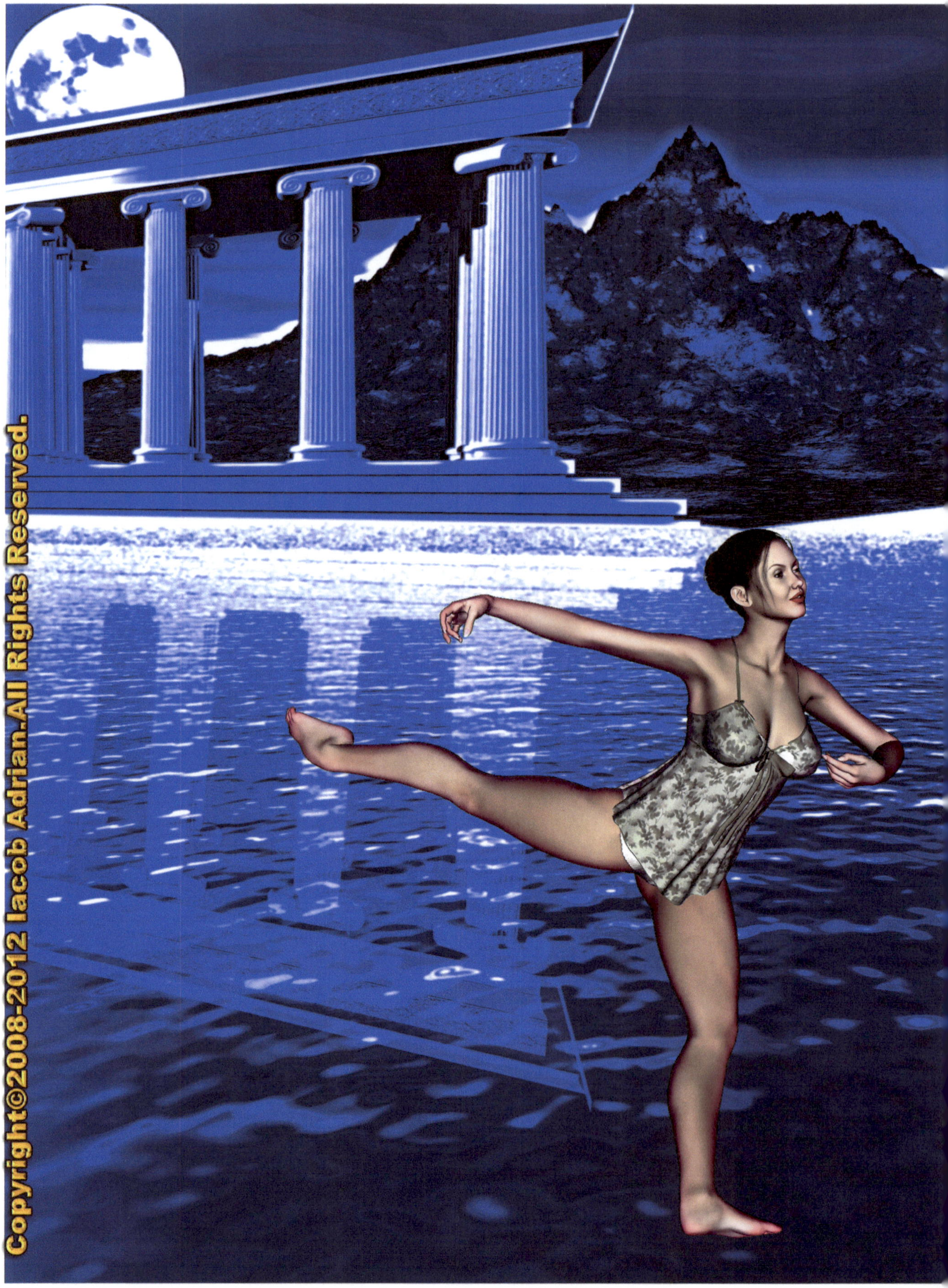
Copyright©2008-2012 Iacob Adrian.All Rights Reserved.

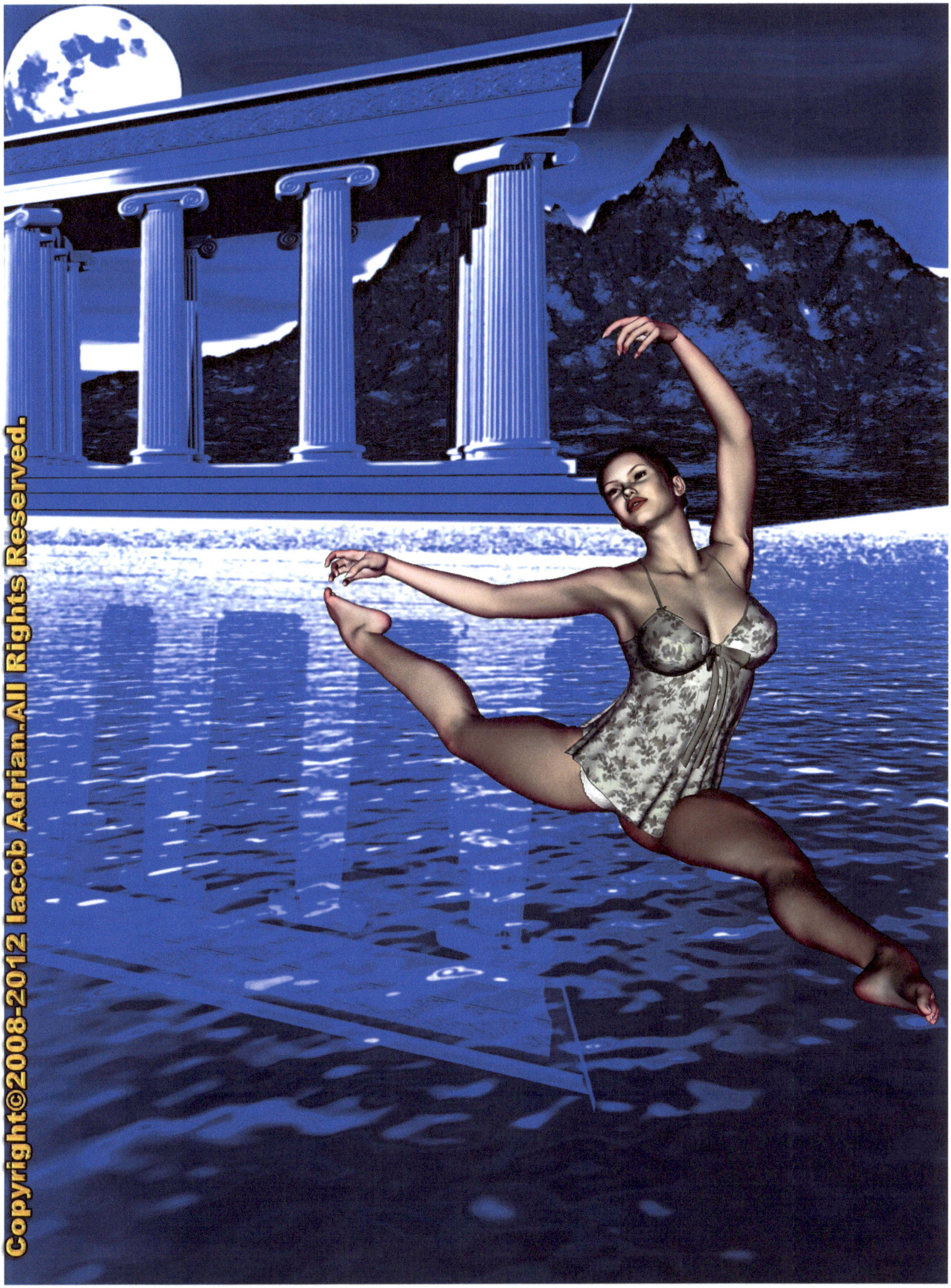
Copyright©2008-2012 Iacob Adrian.All Rights Reserved.

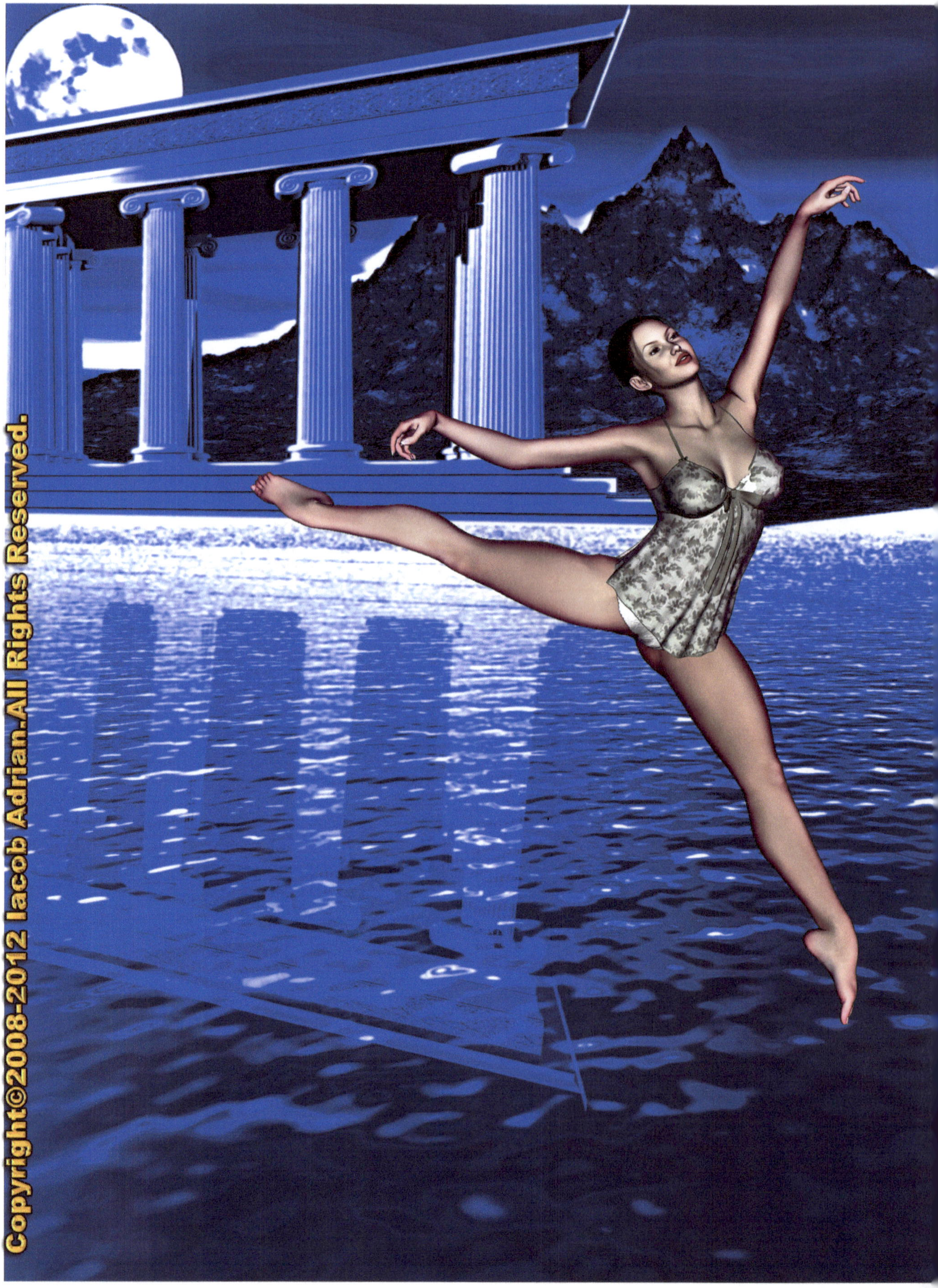
Copyright©2008-2012 Iacob Adrian.All Rights Reserved.

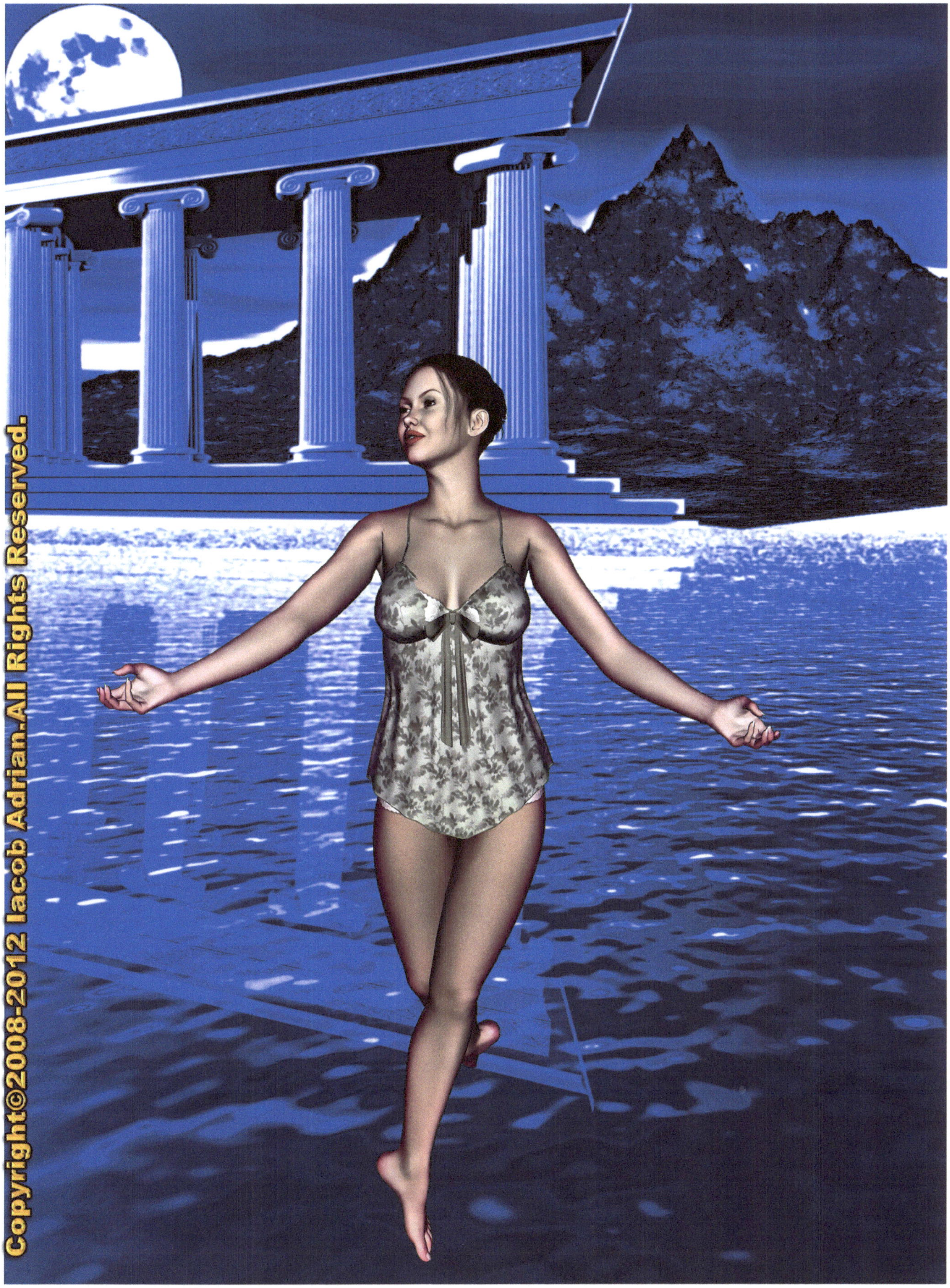
Copyright©2008-2012 Iacob Adrian.All Rights Reserved.

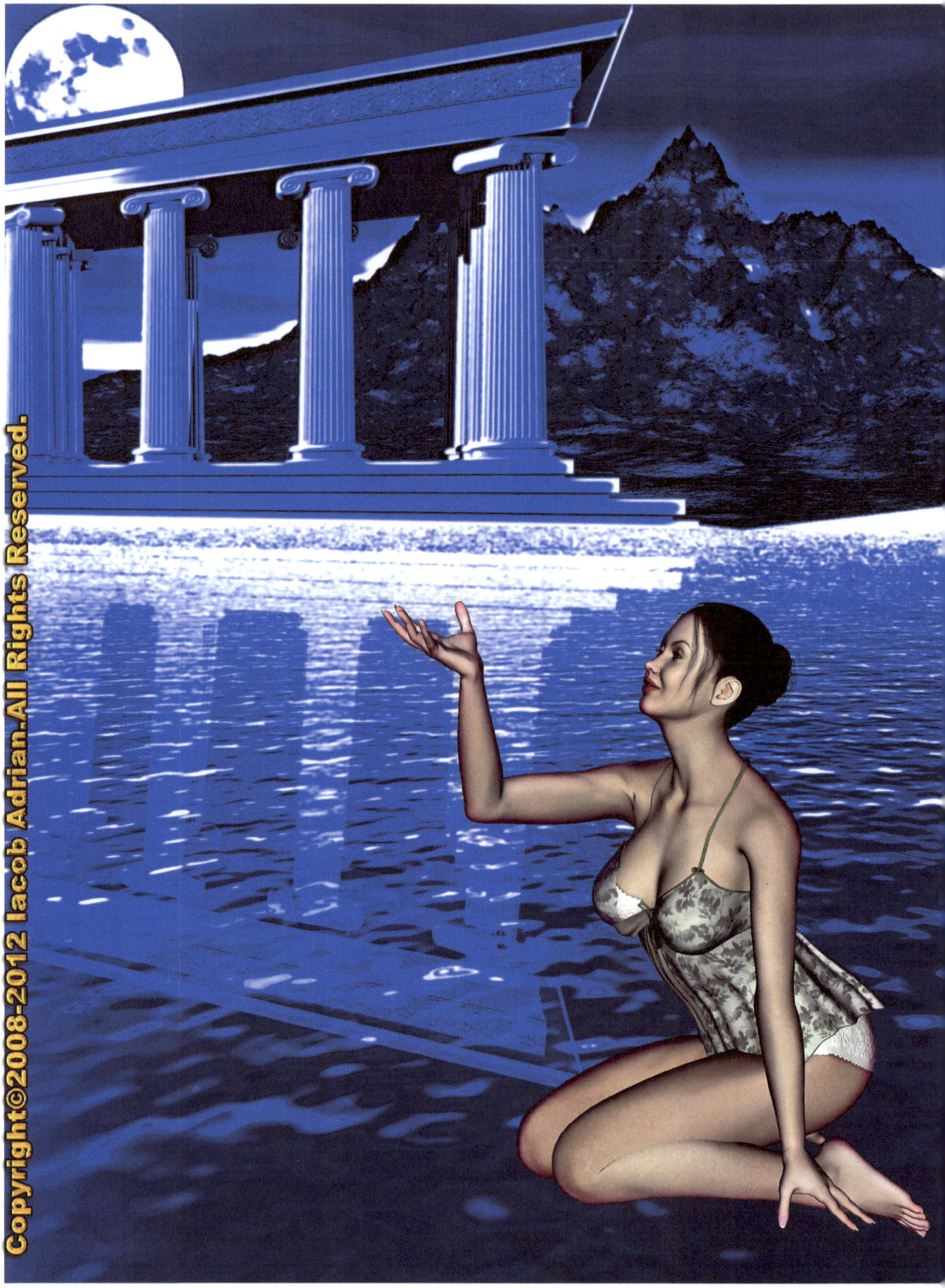
Copyright©2008-2012 Iacob Adrian.All Rights Reserved.

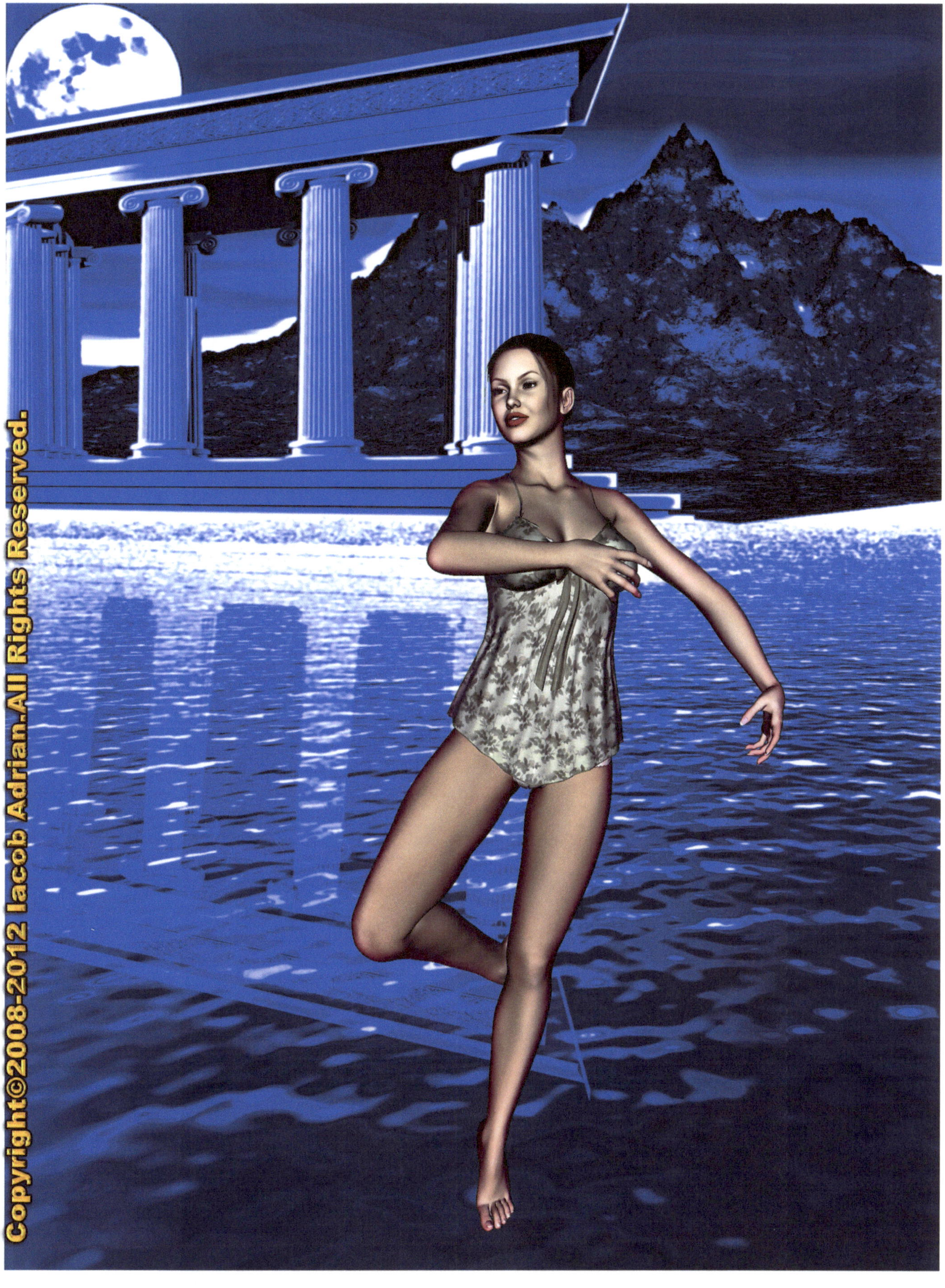

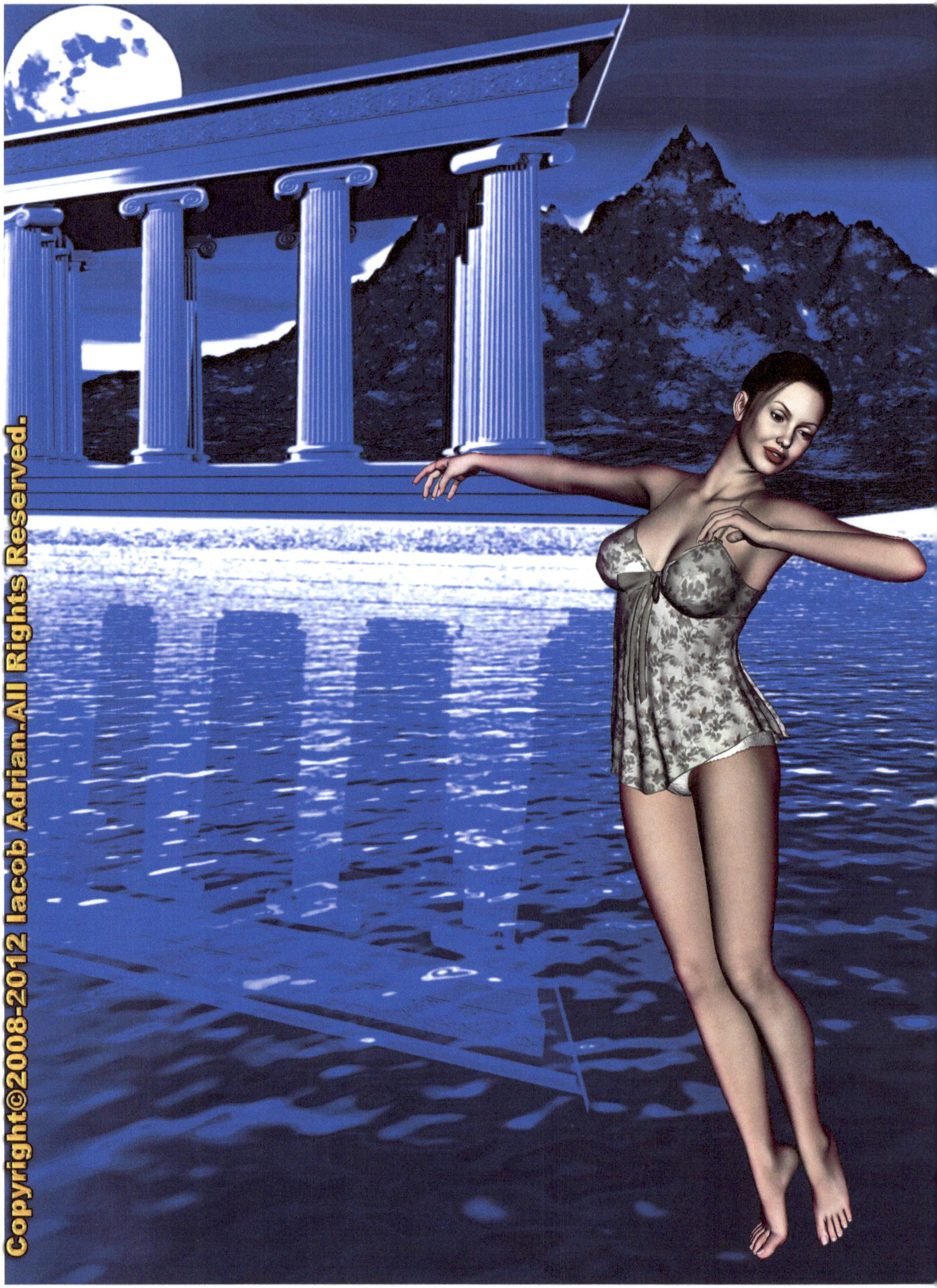
Copyright©2008-2012 Iacob Adrian.All Rights Reserved.

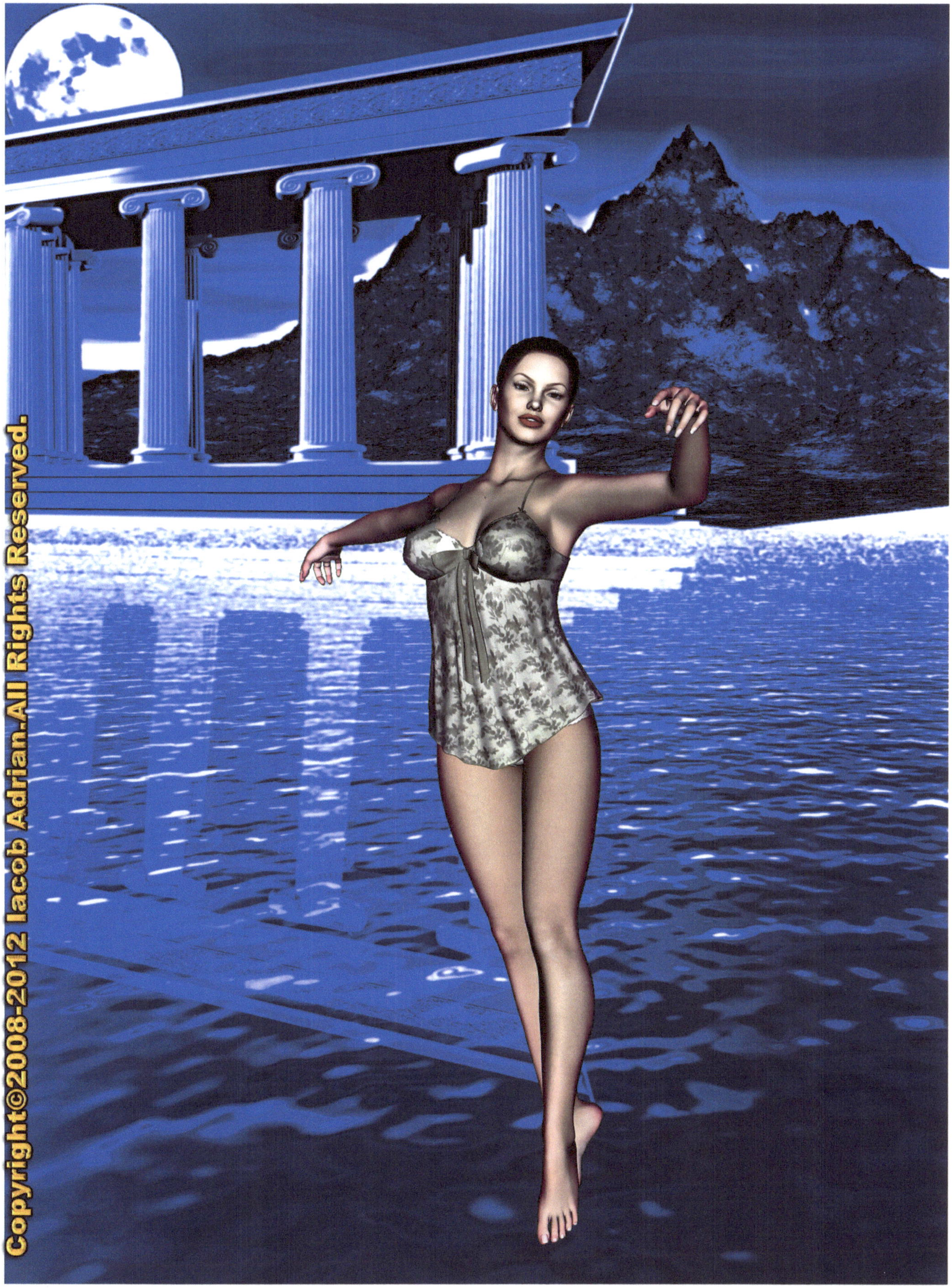

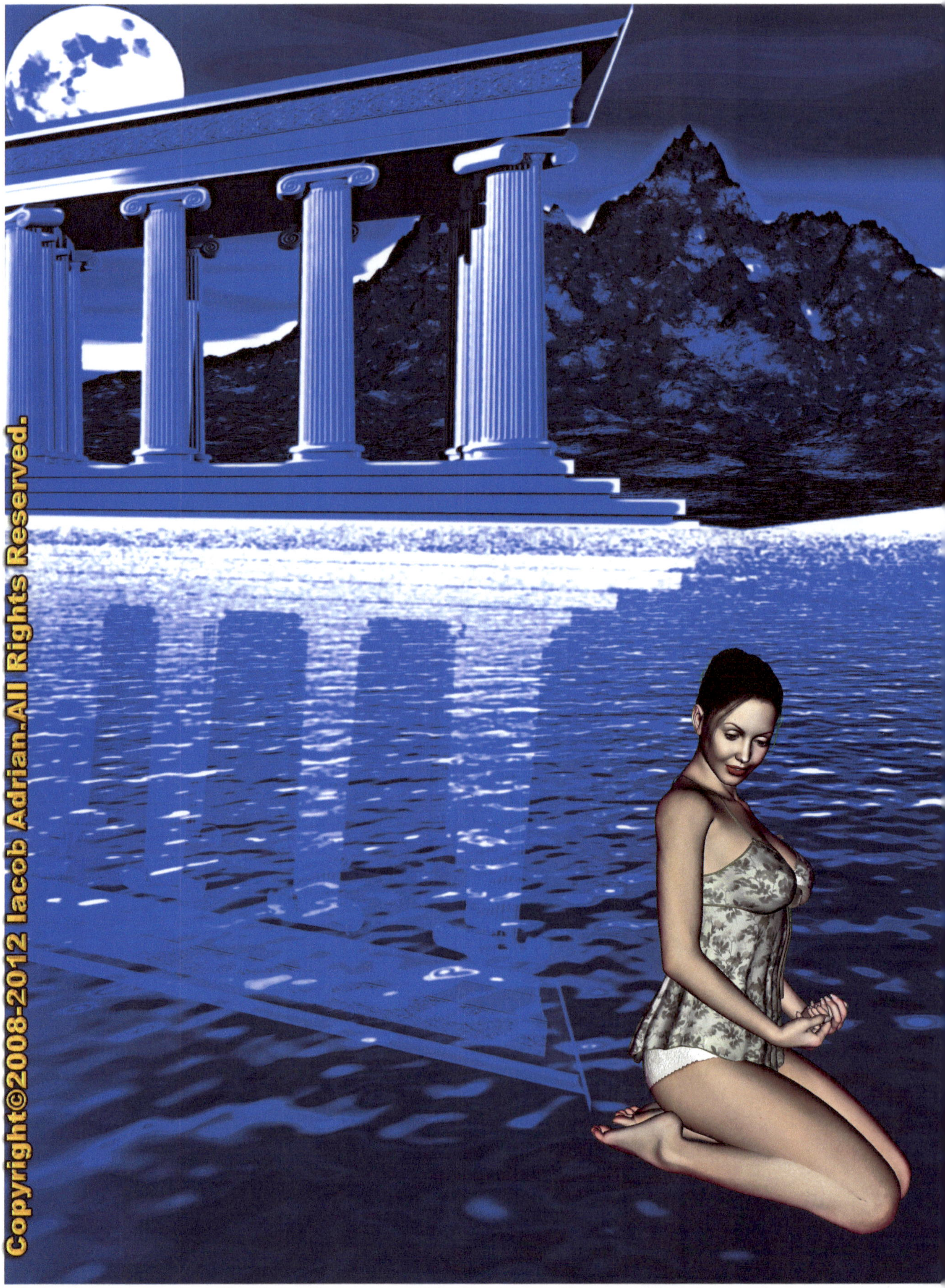

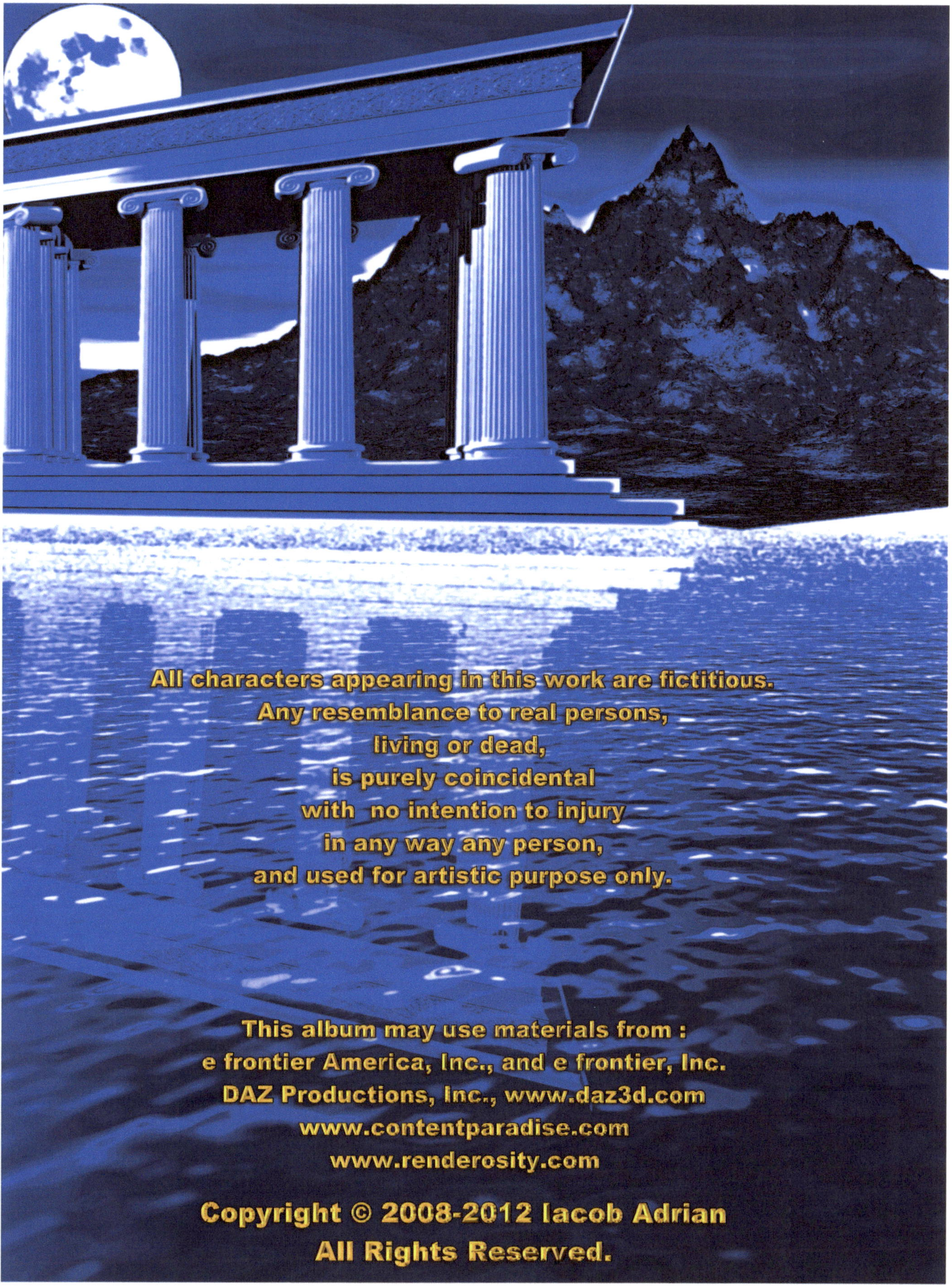

All characters appearing in this work are fictitious.
Any resemblance to real persons,
living or dead,
is purely coincidental
with no intention to injury
in any way any person,
and used for artistic purpose only.

This album may use materials from :
e frontier America, Inc., and e frontier, Inc.
DAZ Productions, Inc., www.daz3d.com
www.contentparadise.com
www.renderosity.com

www.ingramcontent.com/pod-product-compliance
Lightning Source LLC
Chambersburg PA
CBHW041306180526
45172CB00003B/997
* 9 7 8 1 4 7 9 2 3 4 1 2 7 *